A Comparative Study of Mutual Fund's Schemes in India

Vishvnath Y. Borse
(M.Com, NET)

Tajuddin S. Shaikh
(M. Com., LLB)

Rahul M. Revne
(MBA)

CANADIAN
Academic Publishing

2014

Copyright © 2014. Vishvnath Y. Borse, Tajuddin S. Shaikh & Rahul Revne

Price : $27.86

First Edition : 2014

ISBN : 978-1-926488-00-4

ISBN Allotment Agency : Library and Archives Canada (Govt. of Canada)

Published & Printed by

Canadian Academic Publishing
81, Woodlot Crescent,
Etobicoke,
Toronto, Ontario, Canada.
Postal Code- M9W 6T3
Phone- +1 (647) 633 9712
http://www.canadapublish.com

PREFACE

This study has been a great learning experience for us; at the same time it gave us enough scope to implement my analytical ability. This study as a whole can be divided into two parts:

- ❖ The first part gives an insight about the mutual funds and its various aspects. One can have a brief knowledge about mutual funds and all its basics through the project. Other than that the real servings come when one moves ahead. In the 1st part we covered: what are the alternatives of the investing, meaning of the mutual fund, Types of the mutual fund, advantage & dis. advantage of the mutual fund, the structure of the mutual fund & how one can earn from the mutual fund. All the topics have been covered in a very systematic way. The language has been kept simple so that even a layman could understand. All the data's have been well analyzed with the help of charts and graphs.

- ❖ The second part consist the overview of the Reliance & Tata Mutual Fund and the schemes which we used for research with the help of the Sharpe & Treynor Ratio. We also analyzed the company's return for the last couple of ears. Hope the research findings and conclusions will be useful. On the basis of my research & conclusion, we also gave the suggestions which may useful to the company.

CONTENT

Chapter - 1

INTRODUCTION

Savings form an important part of the economy of any nation. With the savings invested in various options available to the people, the money acts as the driver for growth of the country. Indian financial scene too presents a plethora of avenues to the investors. Though certainly not the best or deepest of markets in the world, it has reasonable options for an ordinary man to invest his savings. Banks are considered as the safest of all options, banks have been the roots of the financial systems in India. Promoted as the means to social development, banks in India have indeed played an important role in the rural upliftment. For an ordinary person though, they have acted as the safest investment avenue wherein a person deposits money and earns interest on it. The two main modes of investment in banks, savings accounts and fixed deposits have been effectively used by one and all.

However, today the interest rate structure in the country is headed southwards, keeping in line with global trends. With the banks offering little above 9 percent in their fixed deposits for one year, the yields have come down substantially in recent times. Add to this, the inflationary pressures in economy and one has a position where the savings are not earning. The inflation is creeping up, to almost 8 percent at times, and this means that the value of money saved goes down instead of going up. This effectively mars any chance of gaining from the investments in banks. Just like banks, post offices in India have a wide network. Spread across the nation, they offer financial assistance as well as serving the basic requirements of communication. Among all saving options, Post office schemes have been offering the highest rates. Added to it is the fact that the investments are safe with the department being a Government of India entity. So, the two basic and most sought after features, such as - return safety and quantum of returns was being handsomely taken care of. Though certainly not the most efficient systems in terms of service standards and liquidity, these have still managed to attract the attention of small, retail investors. However, with the government announcing its intention of reducing the interest rates in small savings options, this avenue is expected to lose some of the investors.

Public Provident Funds act as options to save for the post retirement period for most people and have been considered good option largely due to the fact that returns were higher than most other options and also helped people gain from tax benefits under various sections. This option too is likely to lose some of its sheen on account of reduction in the rates offered. Another often-used route to invest has been the fixed deposit schemes floated by companies. Companies have used fixed deposit schemes as a means of mobilizing funds for their operations and have paid interest on them. The safer a company is rated, the lesser the return offered has been the thumb rule. However, there are several potential roadblocks in these. First of all, the danger of financial position of the company not being understood by the investor lurks. The investors rely on intermediaries who more often than not, don't reveal the entire truth. Secondly, liquidity is a major problem with the amount being received months after the due dates. Premature redemption is generally not entertained without cuts in the returns offered and though they present a reasonable option to counter interest rate risk (especially when the economy is headed for a low interest regime), the safety of principal amount has been found lacking. Many cases like the Kuber Group and DCM Group fiascoes have resulted in low confidence in this option. The options discussed above are essentially for the risk-averse, people who think of safety and then quantum of return, in that order. For the brave, it is dabbling in the stock market.

Stock markets provide an option to invest in a high risk, high return game. While the potential return is much more than 10-11 percent any of the options discussed above can generally generate, the risk is undoubtedly of the highest order. But then, the general principle of encountering greater risks and uncertainty when one seeks higher returns holds true. However, as enticing as it might appear, people generally are clueless as to how the stock market functions and in the process can endanger the hard-earned money.

For those who are not adept at understanding the stock market, the task of generating superior returns at similar levels of risk is arduous to say the least. This is where Mutual Funds come into picture.

Mutual Funds are essentially investment vehicles where people with similar investment objective come together to pool their money and then invest accordingly. Each unit of any scheme represents the proportion of pool owned by the unit holder (investor). Appreciation or reduction in value of investments is reflected in net asset value (NAV) of the concerned scheme, which is declared by the fund from time to time. Mutual fund schemes are managed by respective Asset Management Companies (AMC). Different business groups/ financial institutions/ banks have sponsored these AMCs, either alone or in collaboration with reputed international firms.

Several international funds like Alliance and Templeton are also operating independently in India. Many more international Mutual Fund giants are expected to come into Indian markets in the near future.

Investment alternatives in India

1) **Non marketable financial assets**: These are such financial assets which gives moderately high return but cannot be traded in market.
   - Bank Deposits
   - Post Office Schemes
   - Company FDs
   - PPF

2) **Equity shares**: These are shares of company and can be traded in secondary market. Investors get benefit by change in price of share and dividend given by companies. Equity shares represent ownership capital. As an equity shareholder, a person has an ownership stake in the company. This essentially means that the person has a residual interest in income and wealth of the company. These can be classified into following broad categories as per stock market:

- Blue chip shares
- Growth shares
- Income shares
- Cyclic shares
- Speculative shares

3) **Bonds**: Bonds are the instruments that are considered as a relatively safer investment avenues.

- G sec bonds
- GOI relief funds
- Govt. agency funds
- PSU Bonds
- RBI BOND
- Debenture of private sector co.

4) **Money market instrument**: By convention, the term "money market" refers to the market for short-term requirement and deployment of funds. Money market instruments are those instruments, which have a maturity period of less than one year.

- T-Bills
- Certificate of Deposit
- Commercial Paper

5) **Mutual Funds-** A mutual fund is a trust that pools together the savings of a number of investors who share a common financial goal. The fund manager invests this pool of money in securities, ranging from shares, debentures to money market instruments or in a mixture of equity and debt, depending upon the objective of the scheme. The different types of schemes are:

- Balanced Funds
- Index Funds
- Sector Fund
- Equity Oriented Funds

4

6) **Life insurance**: Now-a-days life insurance is also being considered as an investment avenue. Insurance premiums represent the sacrifice and the assured sum the benefit. Under it different schemes are:

> - Endowment assurance policy
> - Money back policy
> - Whole life policy
> - Term assurance policy

7) **Real estate:** One of the most important assets in portfolio of investors is a residential house. In addition to a residential house, the more affluent investors are likely to be interested in the following types of real estate:

> - Agricultural land
> - Semi urban land
> - Farm House

8) **Precious objects**: Investors can also invest in the objects which have value. These comprises of:

> - Gold
> - Silver
> - Precious stones
> - Art objects

9) **Financial Derivatives**: These are such instruments which derive their value from some other underlying assets. It may be viewed as a side bet on the asset. The most important financial derivatives from the point of view of investors are:

> - Options
> - Futures

Chapter - 2

MUTUAL FUND IN INDIA: AN OVERVIEW

A mutual fund is where people invest their money in stocks, bonds, and other securities. Each investor owns shares, which represent a portion of the holdings of the fund. A mutual fund enables investors to pool their money and place it under professional investment management. The portfolio manager trades the fund's underlying securities, realizing a gain or loss, and collects the dividend or interest income. The investment proceeds are then passed along to the individual investors. There are more mutual funds than there are individual stocks.

The first ever mutual fund was set up by the Finance Minister, *T.T. Krishnamachari* who set up the idea of a unit trust that would be "open to any Person or institution to purchase the units offered by the trust.

The industry was one-entity show till 1986 when the UTI monopoly was broken when SBI and Can bank mutual fund entered the arena. This was followed by the entry of others like BOI, LIC, GIC, etc. sponsored by public sector banks. Starting with an asset base of Rs0.25bn in 1964 the industry has grown at a compounded average growth rate of 26.34% to its current size of Rs1130bn. The period 1986-1993 can be termed as the period of public sector mutual funds (PMFs).

Advantages of Investing In Mutual Fund

1)   **Investment Options for different investors and Investment needs:**

   - Debt Funds for regular income
   - Equity Funds for growth of your capital
   - There are various kinds of funds designed to meet different investment needs; Mutual Funds offer investment options ranging from a day to a decade or more.
   - There are options available for the most risk adverse investor and extremely aggressive investor.

- Individuals, Corporate, HUF'S, Trusts and NRI'S can invest and benefit from Mutual Funds.

2) Gain from professional management & risk control

- Mutual Funds are the ideal investment vehicles that allow you to benefit from the market, since they typically offer market linked or above market average returns.
- Mutual Funds are not only managed professionally, but also extensively regulated by SEBI.

3) Liquidity

- Maximum liquidity when compared with any other investment option.

4) Convenience

- Flexibility in the amount of Investment.

- Flexibility in the frequency of Investment.
- Choice of time-horizon of investment: Short Term, Medium Term & Long Term
- Choice of type of Investment: Debt, Equity & Balanced
- Easy to switch between different schemes/ plans (investor can shift from debt to equity markets and from equity to debt).
- Different options available for investments: Dividends & Growth
- Option to invest and withdraw systematically over a period of time.

5) Transparency

- Mutual Fund investing is really simple and transparent.
- Regular updates from fund houses
- Portfolio disclosures necessary as per SEBI regulations.

6) Easy to Buy and Sell

- All it takes is an application form of the fund one wishes to invest in, rest will be taken care by the advisors.
- Redemption request is processed normally within 3 working days.

7) Tax Benefits

- No tax on the dividends in the hands of the investor
- No dividend distribution tax for equity mutual funds (completely tax free dividends).
- Long term capital gains tax benefits

Drawbacks of Mutual Funds

Mutual funds have their drawbacks and may not be for everyone:

1) **No Guarantees:** No investment is risk free. If the entire stock market declines in value, the value of mutual fund shares will go down as well, no matter how balanced the portfolio. Investors encounter fewer risks when they invest in mutual funds than when they buy and sell stocks on their own. However, anyone who invests through a mutual fund runs the risk of losing money.

2) **Fees and commissions:** All funds charge administrative fees to cover their day-to-day expenses. Some funds also charge sales commissions or "loads" to compensate brokers, financial consultants, or financial planners. Even if you don't use a broker or other financial adviser, you will pay a sales commission if you buy shares in a Load Fund.

3) **Management risk:** When anyone invests in a mutual fund, he\she depend on the fund's manager to make the right decisions regarding the fund's portfolio. If the manager does not perform as well as he\she had hoped, he\she might not make as much money on his\her investment as he\she expected. Of course, if he\she invest in Index Funds, you forego management risk, because these funds do not employ managers.

Types of Mutual Fund

Mutual funds can be classified as follow:

A) Based on their structure:

1) **Open-ended Scheme:** An open-ended fund or scheme is one that is available for subscription and repurchase on a continuous basis. These schemes do not have a fixed maturity period. Investors can conveniently buy and sell units at Net Asset Value (NAV) related prices which are declared on a daily basis. The key feature of open-end schemes is liquidity.

2) **Close-ended Scheme:** A close-ended fund or scheme has a stipulated maturity period e.g. 5-7 years. The fund is open for subscription only during a specified period at the time of launch of the scheme. Investors can invest in the scheme at the time of the initial public issue and thereafter they can buy or sell the units of the scheme on the stock exchanges where the units are listed. In order to provide an exit route to the investors, some close-ended funds give an option of selling back the units to the mutual fund through periodic repurchase at NAV related prices. SEBI Regulations stipulate that at least one of the two exit routes is provided to the investor i.e. either repurchase facility or through listing on stock exchanges. These mutual funds schemes disclose NAV generally on weekly basis.

B) Based on their investment objective:

1) **Equity funds:** These funds invest in equities and equity related instruments. With fluctuating share prices, such funds show volatile performance, even losses. However, short term fluctuations in the market, generally smoothens out in the long term, thereby offering higher returns at relatively lower volatility. At the same time, such funds can yield great capital appreciation as, historically, equities have outperformed all asset classes in the long term. Hence, investment in equity funds should be considered for a period of at least 3-5 years. It can be further classified as:

- ➢ Index funds- In this case a key stock market index, like BSE Sensex or Nifty is tracked. Their portfolio mirrors the benchmark index both in terms of composition and individual stock weight ages.
- ➢ Equity diversified funds- 100% of the capital is invested in equities spreading across different sectors and stocks.
- ➢ Dividend yield funds- it is similar to the equity diversified funds except that they invest in companies offering high dividend yields.
- ➢ Thematic funds- Invest 100% of the assets in sectors which are related through some theme. For example an infrastructure fund invests in power, construction, cements sectors etc.
- ➢ Sector funds- Invest 100% of the capital in a specific sector. e.g. - A banking sector fund will invest in banking stocks.
- ➢ ELSS- Equity Linked Saving Scheme provides tax benefit to the investors.

2) **Balanced fund:** Their investment portfolio includes both debt and equity. As a result, on the risk-return ladder, they fall between equity and debt funds. Balanced funds are the ideal mutual funds vehicle for investors who prefer spreading their risk across various instruments. Following are balanced funds classes:
- ➢ Debt-oriented funds -Investment below 65% in equities.
- ➢ Equity-oriented funds -Invest at least 65% in equities, remaining in debt.

3) **Debt fund:** They invest only in debt instruments, and are a good option for investors averse to idea of taking risk associated with equities. Therefore, they invest exclusively in fixed-income instruments like bonds, debentures, Government of India securities; and money market instruments such as certificates of deposit (CD), commercial paper (CP) and call money. Put your money into any of these debt funds depending on your investment horizon and needs.
- ➢ Liquid funds- These funds invest 100% in money market instruments, a large portion being invested in call money market.

- Gilt funds ST- They invest 100% of their portfolio in government securities of and T-bills.
- Floating rate funds - Invest in short-term debt papers. Floaters invest in debt instruments which have variable coupon rate.
- Arbitrage fund- They generate income through arbitrage opportunities due to mis-pricing between cash market and derivatives market. Funds are allocated to equities, derivatives and money markets. Higher proportion (around 75%) is put in money markets, in the absence of arbitrage opportunities.
- Gilt funds LT- They invest 100% of their portfolio in long-term government securities.
- Income funds LT- Typically; such funds invest a major portion of the portfolio in long-term debt papers.
- MIPs- Monthly Income Plans have an exposure of 70%-90% to debt and an exposure of 10%-30% to equities.
- FMPs- fixed monthly plans invest in debt papers whose maturity is in line with that of the fund.

Mutual Fund Structure

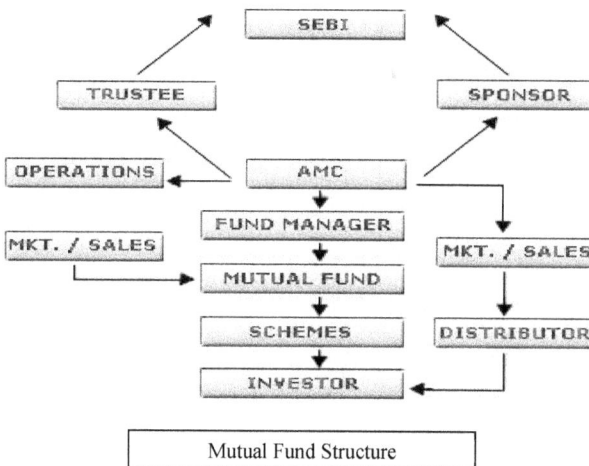

Mutual Fund Structure

The structure consists of:

1) **Sponsor:** Sponsor is the person who acting alone or in combination with another body corporate establishes a mutual fund. Sponsor must contribute at least 40% of the net worth of the Investment Managed and meet the eligibility criteria prescribed under the Securities and Exchange Board of India (Mutual Funds) Regulations, 1996.The Sponsor is not responsible or liable for any loss or shortfall resulting from the operation of the Schemes beyond the initial contribution made by it towards setting up of the Mutual Fund.

2) **Trust:** The Mutual Fund is constituted as a trust in accordance with the provisions of the Indian Trusts Act, 1882 by the Sponsor. The trust deed is registered under the Indian Registration Act, 1908.

3) **Trustee:** Trustee is usually a company (corporate body) or a Board of Trustees (body of individuals). The main responsibility of the Trustee is to safeguard the interest of the unit holders and inter alia ensure that the AMC functions in the interest of investors and in accordance with the Securities and Exchange Board of India (Mutual Funds) Regulations, 1996, the provisions of the Trust Deed and the Offer Documents of the respective Schemes. At least 2/3rd directors of the Trustee are independent directors who are not associated with the Sponsor in any manner.

4) **Asset Management Company (AMC):** The AMC is appointed by the Trustee as the Investment Manager of the Mutual Fund. The AMC is required to be approved by the Securities and Exchange Board of India (SEBI) to act as an asset management company of the Mutual Fund. At least 50% of the directors of the AMC are independent directors who are not associated with the Sponsor in any manner. The AMC must have a net worth of at least 10 crore at all times.

5) **Registrar and Transfer Agent:** The AMC if so authorized by the Trust Deed appoints the Registrar and Transfer Agent to the Mutual Fund. The Registrar processes the application form, redemption requests and dispatches account

statements to the unit holders. The Registrar and Transfer agent also handles communications with investors and updates investor records.

How one can earn wealth from Mutual Funds?

One can earn money from your investment in three ways:

1) **Dividend Payments**: A fund may earn income in the form of dividends and interest on the securities in its portfolio. The fund then pays its shareholders nearly all of the income (minus disclosed expenses) it has earned in the form of dividends.
2) **Capital Gains Distributions**: The price of the securities a fund owns may increase. When a fund sells a security that has increased in price, the fund has a capital gain. At the end of the year, most funds distribute these capital gains (minus any capital losses) to investors.
3) **Increased NAV**: If the market value of a fund's portfolio increases after deduction of expenses and liabilities, then the value (NAV) of the fund and its shares increases. The higher NAV reflects the higher value of his\her investment.

Some additional facilities provided by mutual fund:

1) **Systematic Investment Plan (SIP):** This is an investment technique where you deposit a fixed, small amount regularly into the mutual fund scheme (every month or quarter as per your convenience) at the then prevailing NAV (Net Asset Value), subject to applicable load.
2) **Systematic withdrawal plan (SWP):** Under a systematic withdrawal plan, an investor can receive regular/quarterly payments from the scheme in to his account. The Unit holder can opt to withdraw a fixed amount subject to a prescribed minimum amount per month or per quarter.
3) **Systematic Transfer plan (STP):** A systematic transfer plan, investor can choose to transfer their dividends of scheme to another scheme at periodic intervals.

4) **Dividend Transfer Plan (DTP):** Under dividend transfer plan, investors can choose to transfer their dividends of one scheme on to the other scheme as an when dividends are paid out. If such a plan is chosen than the amount of dividend distribution will be automatically invested on the ex-dividend date into the scheme selected by the investor and units will be allotted accordingly.

5) **Auto Debit facility and Electronic clearing service:** A systematic investment plan can be affected in two ways. The investor can postdated cheques dated at requisite intervals or investor can choose for an auto debit facility / ECS. In this facility, the account mentioned in his application form would be automatically debited on the date of investment and amount would be invested in the scheme.

6) **Switch**: Unit have an option to switch all or part of their investment in one scheme plan to another scheme plan established by the fund that is available for investment at that time. The switch will be affected by way of redemption of unit and a re-investment of the redemption proceeds in another scheme.

Chapter - 3

REVIEW OF LITERATURE

The present study deals with the review of literature on 'Evaluating the Performance of Indian Mutual Fund Schemes'. A number of studies on evaluating the performance of Indian Mutual Fund Schemes have been conducted in India and foreign countries. Review of some of the studies is presented in the following discussion: -

Treynor (1965) and Sharpe (1966) have provided the conceptual framework of relative measure of performance of equity mutual funds while Treynor used systematic risk. Sharpe used total risk to evaluate the mutual fund portfolio performance higher value of Treynor's index indicates better performance of portfolio and vice versa.

Gupta LC (1981) presented a detailed and well-based estimate of "Portfolio" rate of return on equities. This pioneering study in the Indian context has been a major contribution in this field and is regarded as the benchmark on the rate of return on equities for the specified time. He laid the basis of rate of return concept in performance evaluation.

Jain (1982) evaluated performance of unit trust of India (UTI) during 1964-65 to 1979-80, including the profitability aspects of unit scheme 1964, unit scheme 1971 and unit scheme 1976. He concluded that its real rate of return have been low indicating overall poor, performance of UTI Schemes. There has been so significant increase in the profitability over the years.

Henriksson (1984) evaluated performance in terms of market timing abilities with sample of 116 open ended investment schemes during the period, February 1968, June 1980. The empirical results obtained indicated unsatisfactory timing skills of the fund managers.

Holthausen (1992) have developed a model based on 60 financial ratios that predicts return over 12 month's period. The study was found particularly useful predictor of stock prices and can be useful in fundamental analysis while taking equity investment decisions.

Daniel (1997) has concluded that the 'persistence in mutual funds Results show that particularly aggressive growth funds exhibit some "selectivity" ability but no "timing ability."

The Research on "Performance Evaluation of Indian Mutual Funds" was done by Dr S Narayan Rao in IITB (2002). The Study is conducted to understand whether most of the mutual fund schemes were able to satisfy investor's expectations by giving excess returns over expected returns.

Sharpe (1966) suggested a measure for the evaluation of portfolio performance. Drawing on results obtained in the field of portfolio analysis. Economist Jack L Treynor suggested a new predictor of mutual fund performance, one that differs from virtually all those used previously by incorporating the volatility of a funds return in a simple yet meaningful manner.

Ippolito R.A. (1992) concluded that the investors prefer mutual funds which have a record of positive return in the past .

Jayadev (1996) evaluated the performance of two growth-oriented mutual funds namely Mastergain and Magnum express by using monthly returns. Jensen, Sharpe and Treynor measures have been applied in the study and the pointed out that according to Jensen and Treynor measure Mastergain have performed better and the performance of Magnum was poor according to all three measures.

Sapar & Narayan(2003) evaluates the performance of 269 open ended schemes of mutual funds in a bear market using relative performance index, risk-return analysis, Treynor's ratio, Sharp's ratio, Sharp's measure, Jensen's measure, and Fama's. The results obtained advocate that most of the mutual fund schemes in

16

the sample outperformed the investor's expectations by giving excess return over expected return based on premium for systematic risk and total risk.

Rao D. N (2006) studied the financial performance of select open-ended equity mutual fund schemes for the period 1st April 2005 - 31st March 2006 pertaining to the two dominant investment styles and tested the hypothesis whether the differences in performance are statistically significant. The analysis indicated that growth plans have generated higher returns than that of dividend plans but at a higher risk studied classified the 419 open-ended equity mutual fund schemes into six distinct investment styles.

Chapter - 4

RESEARCH METHODOLOGY

Objectives:

The major objectives of study are as follows.

- ➤ To evaluate investment performance of mutual funds in terms of risk and return.
- ➤ To examine the funds sensitivity to the market fluctuations in terms of beta.
- ➤ To find out the financial performance of mutual fund schemes.
- ➤ To appraise investment performance of mutual funds with risk adjustment, the theoretical parameters as suggested by Sharpe, Treynor and Jensen.
- ➤ To analyze the performance of various schemes of mutual funds.
- ➤ To identify the sector where the mutual fund and how invested.
- ➤ To provide valuable suggestions and recommendations.

Scope of the Study:

The study of mutual fund has the wider scope. Mutual fund is a professionally managed form of collective investment that pools money from many investors and invest it in stocks, bonds, short-term money market instruments and other securities. Mutual fund distributors of tax free municipal bonds income are also tax free to the share holders. Taxable distribution can be either ordinary income or capital schemes which are equity schemes, debt and hybrid schemes.

Selection of Companies:

The present study includes five-year return of the mutual fund companies and funds in India. Out of all mutual fund companies we have selected only two companies those are **RELIANCE MUTUAL FUND and TATA MUTUAL FUND**, and only those schemes and funds are included in this study, which are performed well during from last few years.

Methodology:

Methodology is a way to systematically solve the research problem. It may be understood as a science of studying how research is done scientifically. In it we study the various steps that are generally adopted by a research in studying his research problem along with the logic behind them. Methodology refers to methods adopted to carry out the research and steps adopted to solve the problem finding solution

Type of the study:

The type of the study or research used in this project is a descriptive research design. It mainly involves surveys and facts findings enquiries of different kinds. The main objective of descriptive research is to describe the state of affairs as it exists at present. The major purpose of descriptive research is a description of the state of the affairs, as it exists at present. Thus a descriptive study is a fact finding investigation with adequate interpretation. It is the simplest type of research. It focuses on particular aspects or dimensions of the problem studied. It is designed that it gathers descriptive information and provides information for formulating more sophisticated studies. There is a cause effective relationship.

The criteria for selecting this particular design are that, the problem of the project must be described and not arguable. The data collected is amenable to statistical analysis and has accuracy and significance. It is possible to develop to valid standards of comparison. It tends itself to the verifiable procedure of collection and analysis of data.

Descriptive study objective aim at identifying the various characteristics of a company problem under study. It can reveal potential relationships between variables with exploratory research.

Type of data:

The data which is used for the research is secondary data. The secondary data is the data which is duplicate of primary data. "The data (published or unpublished)

which have already been collected and processed by some agency or person and taken over from there and used by any other agency for their statistical work are termed as person and taken over from there are termed as secondary data" as far as second agency is concerned. The second agency if and when it publishes and files such data becomes the secondary source to anyone who later uses these data.

In other words, secondary source is the agency who publishes for use by others the data which was not originally collected and processed by it.

Tools for analysis:

1) **Standard deviation**: It is used to measure the variation in individual returns from the average expected return over a certain period. Standard deviation is used in the concept of risk of a portfolio of investments; higher standard deviation means a greater fluctuation in expected return.

2) **Beta:** Beta measures the systematic risk and shows how prices of securities respond to the market forces. It is calculated by relating the return on a security with return for the market. By convention, market will have beta 1.0 Mutual fund is said to be volatile, more volatile or less volatile. If beta is greater than 1 the stock is said to be riskier than market. If beta is less than 1, the indication is that stock is less risky in comparison to market. If beta is zero then the risk is the same as that of the market. Negative beta is rare.

3) **Sharpe index:** Sharpe Ratio is a tool to measure the performance of mutual funds over a period of time.

$$Sharpe\ Index = \frac{Portfolio\ Average\ Return\ (R_p) - Risk\ Free\ Rate\ of\ Interest\ (R_t)}{Standard\ Deviations\ of\ the\ Portfolio\ Return}$$

This measure takes into account surplus return earned by the fund over risk free rate of interest and then divides it by standard deviation of the portfolio return.

4) Treynor's Index: Treynor's model is on the concept of the characteristics straight line. This ratio also takes into account surplus return earned over risk free return but the measure of risk here is beta rather than standard deviation. Thus the emphasis is more on market risk (systematic risk) rather than deviation of returns from the mean. It should be noted that this measure

ignores the unsystematic risk or risk which is typical to a particular security. This measure is more relevant as unsystematic risk is negligible in overall portfolio of a mutual fund (or at least supposed to be) and hence it is feasible to judge performance of a fund from this measure.

$$Treynor's\ Index = \frac{Portfolio\ Average\ Return\ (R_p) - Avg.\ Risk\ Free\ Rate\ of\ Interest\ (R_t)}{Beta\ Coefficient\ of\ Portfolio}$$

Chapter - 5
PROFILE OF SELECTED COMPANIES

A)   Tata Mutual Fund

The Tata Asset Management philosophy is centered on seeking consistent, long-term results. When one chooses to invest with Tata Mutual Fund, he/she will get the benefits of financial planning. Tata Asset Management aims at overall excellence, within the framework of transparent and rigorous risk controls.

Tata Asset Management Ltd. constantly benchmarks its efforts against these tenets of performance.

The Tata name is a unique asset representing leadership with trust. Leveraging this asset to enhance Group synergy and becoming globally competitive is the route to sustained growth and long-term success.

Tata Five Core Values

The Tata Group has always sought to be a value-driven organization. These values continue to direct the Group's growth and businesses. The five core Tata values underpinning the way we do business are:

➤ **Integrity:** We must conduct our business fairly, with honesty and transparency. Everything we do must stand the test of public scrutiny.

➤ **Understanding:** We must be caring, show respect, compassion and humanity for our colleagues and customers around the world, and always work for the benefit of the communities we serve.

➤ **Excellence:** We must constantly strive to achieve the highest possible standards in our day-to-day work and in the quality of the goods and services we provide

➤ **Unity:** We must work cohesively with our colleagues across the Group and with our customers and partners around the world, building strong relationships based on tolerance, understanding and mutual cooperation.

> **Responsibility:** We must continue to be responsible, sensitive to the countries, communities and environments in which we work, always ensuring that what comes from the people goes back to the people many times over.

Types of Tata Mutual Fund:

1) **Tata Infrastructure Fund**

Objective

To provide income distribution and / Or medium to long term capital gains by investing predominantly in equity / equity related instrument of companies in infrastructure sector.

Fund Features

Type of Scheme	Open Ended
Nature	Equity
Option	Growth
Inception Date	Dec 22, 2004
Face Value (Rs/Unit)	10
Fund Size in Rs. Cr.	2046.55 as on Sep 30, 2008
Fund Manager	M Venugopal .
SIP	✓
STP	✓
SWP	✓
Expense ratio (%)	2.25
Portfolio Turnover Ratio (%)	52.69

The said scheme is open ended scheme, so, investor can sell and purchase the units at any time. In this scheme, SIP, STP & SWP, all options are available for investment.

Top 10 Holdings:

Stock	Sector
Nifty	Miscellaneous
Larsen & Toubro Limited	Engineering & Industrial Machinery
Reliance Industries Ltd	Oil & Gas, Petroleum & Refinery
Bharat Heavy Electricals Ltd	Electricals & Electrical Equipments
Oil & Natural Gas Corp. Ltd	Oil & Gas, Petroleum & Refinery
HDFC Bank Ltd	Banks
Bharti Airtel Ltd	Telecom
ICICI BANK LTD.	Banks
Punjab National Bank	Banks
Crompton Greaves Ltd	Electricals & Electrical Equipments

Sector Allocation (%)

Sector	%
Banks	13.61
Cement	2.00
Consumer Durables	0.69
Current Assets	11.53
Electricals & Electrical Equipments	7.79
Engineering & Industrial Machinery	9.67
Finance	2.26
Housing & Construction	5.87
Metals	1.06
Miscellaneous	15.22
Oil & Gas, Petroleum & Refinery	12.78
Power Generation, Transmission & Equip	5.85

Shipping	0.86
Steel	7.09
Telecom	3.72

As per above table, we can see that the major part of the amount has been invested in "Miscellaneous" i.e., Nifty. So, we can say that fund manager was risk taker and want to take some risk through NIFTY. Another portion has been invested in banking sector and i.e., 13.61and third portion has been invested in "Oil & Gas, Petroleum & Refinery" and I.e., 12.78.

Asset Allocation

Equity	Debt	Cash & Equivalent
88.47	0.00	11.53

Here, asset allocation for the port folio is 88.47 in equity & 11.53 in Cash & Equivalent. So, we can say that risk taking capacity is higher and investor also get the good return also..vis a vis.

2)   **Tata Equity P/E Fund**

Objective

To provide reasonable & regular income along with possible capital appreciation to its unit holders.

Fund Features

Type of Scheme	Open Ended
Nature	Equity
Option	Growth
Inception Date	June 15,2004
Face Value (Rs/Unit)	10
Fund Size in Rs. Cr.	120.43 as on Sep 30, 2008
Fund Manager	Bhupinder Sethi
SIP	✓
STP	✓
SWP	✓
Expense Ratio(%)	2.42
Portfolio Turnover Ratio (%)	73.76

The said scheme is open ended scheme, so, investor can sell and purchase the units at any time. In this scheme, SIP, STP & SWP, all options are available for investment.

Sector Weightings

Sector	%
Auto & Auto ancilliaries	8.07
Banks	17.71
Cement	1.64
Computers – Hardware	1.28
Computers - Software & Education	6.10
Current Assets	6.26
Electronics	0.81
Engineering & Industrial Machinery	1.52

Entertainment	9.44
Fertilizers, Pesticides & Agrochemicals	1.88
Finance	3.49
Metals	8.87
Mining & Minerals	1.40
Miscellaneous	2.05
Oil & Gas, Petroleum & Refinery	8.87
Paints	1.19
Pharmaceuticals	3.95
Shipping	1.76
Steel	8.62
Tea	3.06
Transport & Travel	2.04

As per above table, we can see that the major part of the amount has been invested in "Bank" means one can invest in this scheme then he can expect some amount of return. Then another big investment in "Entertainment" sector so, we can say that fund manager was risk taker but he is taking the risk systematically.

Assets Allocation (%)

Equity	Debt	Cash & Equivalent
86.63	0.00	13.37

Here also asset allocation for portfolio higher in equity (86.47) which indicate higher risk taking capacity.

3) **Tata Contra Fund**

Objective

        The investment objective of the Scheme is to provide income distribution and/or medium to long term capital gains while at all times emphasizing the importance of capital appreciation. However there is no assurance that the investment objective of the scheme will be achieved.

Fund Features

Type of Scheme	**Open Ended**
Nature	Equity
Option	Growth
Inception Date	Oct 25, 2005
Face Value (Rs/Unit)	10
Fund Size in Rs. Cr.	94.55 as on Sep 30, 2008
Fund Manager	Bhupinder Sethi .
SIP	✓
STP	✓
SWP	✓
Expense ratio(%)	2.44
Portfolio Turnover Ratio(%)	119.98

The said scheme is open ended scheme, so, investor can sell and purchase the units at any time. In this scheme, SIP, STP & SWP, all options are available for investment.

Top 10 Holdings

Stock	Sector
HDFC Bank Ltd	Banks
Indian Hotels Co Ltd	Hotels & Resorts
3M India Ltd.	Trading

ICICI BANK LTD.	Banks
Hindalco Industries Ltd	Metals
Nestle India Ltd	Food & Dairy Products
Bharat Heavy Electricals Ltd	Electricals & Electrical Equipments
Balaji Telefilms Ltd	Entertainment
Hindustan Petroleum Corporation Ltd	Oil & Gas, Petroleum & Refinery
Power Grid Corporation of India Ltd	Power Generation, Transmission & Equip

Sector Allocation

Sector	%
Auto & Auto ancilliaries	1.90
Banks	14.60
Cement	1.52
Computers – Hardware	0.54
Computers - Software & Education	3.18
Consumer Durables	0.73
Current Assets	3.46
Electricals & Electrical Equipments	3.35
Electronics	1.04
Engineering & Industrial Machinery	1.75
Entertainment	6.49
Fertilizers, Pesticides & Agrochemicals	4.06
Finance	4.72
Food & Dairy Products	3.96
Hotels & Resorts	7.88

Housing & Construction	3.13
Metals	6.44
Miscellaneous	3.41
Oil & Gas, Petroleum & Refinery	8.47
Pharmaceuticals	3.65
Power Generation, Transmission & Equip	6.32
Steel	4.19
Tea	2.13
Trading	1.52
Transport & Travel	1.57

As per above table, we can see that the major part of the amount has been invested in "Bank" means one can invest in this scheme then he can expect some amount of return. Here we can see that, investment most of the is done in volatile sector, so, it might be possible that, investor can get huge amount of return else he might be received loss also.

Asset Allocation

Equity	Debt	Cash & Equivalent
96.54	0.00	3.46

Here, asset allocation is 96.54 in equity in 3.46 in Cash & Equivalent. So, It's easy to say that fund manager is taking the higher risk against the portfolio and as per finance rule, risk and return is always high. So, the expected return and loss is always high.

B)   Reliance Mutual Fund

The Reliance group - one of India's largest business houses with revenues of Rs. 990 billion ($22.6 billion) that is equal to 3.5 percent of the country's gross domestic product was split into two.

The group - which claims to contribute nearly 10 per cent of the country's indirect tax revenues and over six percent of India's exports - was divided between Mukesh Ambani and his younger brother Anil on June 18, 2005.

The group's activities span exploration, production, refining and marketing of oil and natural gas, petrochemicals, textiles, financial services, insurance, power and telecom. The family also has interests in advertising agency and life sciences.

Reliance Mutual Fund (RMF) is one of India's leading Mutual Funds, with Average Assets Under Management (AAUM) of Rs. 88616 Crores (AAUM for 31st Aug 08) and an investor base of over 69.21 Lacs.

Reliance Mutual Fund, a part of the Reliance - Anil Dhirubhai Ambani Group, is one of the fastest growing mutual funds in the country. RMF offers investors a well-rounded portfolio of products to meet varying investor requirements and has presence in 118 cities across the country.

Reliance Mutual Fund constantly endeavors to launch innovative products and customer service initiatives to increase value to investors.

"Reliance Mutual Fund schemes are managed by Reliance Capital Asset Management Limited., a subsidiary of Reliance Capital Limited, which holds 93.37% of the paid-up capital of RCAM, the balance paid up capital being held by minority shareholders."

Reliance Capital Ltd. is one of India's leading and fastest growing private sector financial services companies, and ranks among the top 3 private sector financial services and banking companies, in terms of net worth.

Reliance Capital Ltd. has interests in asset management, life and general insurance, private equity and proprietary investments, stock broking and other financial services.

Types of Reliance Mutual Fund:

1) **Reliance Growth Fund**

INVESTMENT OBJECTIVE

Seeks to provide Long Term Capital Appreciation

Fund Features

Type of Scheme	Open Ended
Nature	Equity
Option	Growth
Inception Date	Oct 7, 1995
Face Value (Rs/Unit)	10
Fund Size in Rs. Cr.	4337.02 as on Sep 30, 2008
Fund Manager	Sunil Singhania .
SIP	✓
STP	✓
SWP	✓
Expense ratio(%)	1.81
Portfolio Turnover Ratio(%)	48

The said scheme is open ended scheme, so, investor can sell and purchase the units at any time. In this scheme, SIP, STP & SWP, all options are available for investment.

Top 10 Holdings

Stock	Sector
Other Equities	Miscellaneous
Divis Laboratories Limited	Pharmaceuticals
Jindal Steel and Power Ltd.	Steel

Reliance Industries Ltd	Oil & Gas, Petroleum & Refinery
Jindal Saw Ltd.	Steel
Lupin Ltd.	Pharmaceuticals
Bank of Baroda	Banks
Gujarat Mineral Development Corporation Limited	Mining & Minerals
Adani Enterprises Ltd	Trading
Reliance Communication Ventures Ltd.	Telecom

Sector Allocation

Sector	%
Auto & Auto ancilliaries	1.53
Banks	7.57
Breweries & Distilleries	1.06
Chemicals	1.20
Computers - Software & Education	1.45
Current Assets	26.69
Electricals & Electrical Equipments	1.27
Engineering & Industrial Machinery	2.78
Fertilizers, Pesticides & Agrochemicals	3.05
Food & Dairy Products	1.28
Housing & Construction	1.81
Mining & Minerals	1.44
Miscellaneous	18.49
Oil & Gas, Petroleum & Refinery	5.24
Paper	1.13

Pharmaceuticals	7.63
Plastic	3.91
Power Generation, Transmission & Equip	1.37
Steel	5.96
Telecom	3.34
Trading	1.78

Here, the main investment in nifty, bank, still & oil-gas companies. So, we can say that investment is under the volatile sector. Risk factor is always high, in the said scheme.

Asset Allocation

Equity	Debt	Cash & Equivalent
73.31	0.00	26.69

Here we can see that the ratio of the asset allocation is 73:26 in equity & cash, So, we can assume that chances of accruing loss is less. From Sector allocation, we can see that, investment has been done in those scheme which are less volatile. SO, One can expect return in a long term.

2)   **Reliance Vision Fund**

Objective

Seeks to provide long term capital appreciation primarily investing in growth oriented stocks.

Fund Features

Type of Scheme	**Open Ended**
Nature	Equity
Option	Growth
Inception Date	Aug 8, 2007
Face Value (Rs/Unit)	10
Fund Size in Rs. Cr.	3032.04 as on Sep 30, 2008
Fund Manager	Ashwani Kumar .
SIP	✗
STP	✗
SWP	✗
Expense ratio(%)	1.64
Portfolio Turnover Ratio(%)	87

The said scheme is open ended scheme, so, investor can sell and purchase the units at any time. In this scheme, SIP, STP & SWP, all options are not available for investment.

Top 10 Holdings

Stock	Sector
Divis Laboratories Limited	Pharmaceuticals
Reliance Industries Ltd	Oil & Gas, Petroleum & Refinery
Other Equities	Miscellaneous
ICICI BANK LTD.	Banks
State Bank of India	Banks
Larsen & Toubro Limited	Engineering & Industrial Machinery

Reliance Communication Ventures Ltd.	Telecom
Maruti Udyog Ltd	Auto & Auto ancilliaries
Oil & Natural Gas Corp. Ltd	Oil & Gas, Petroleum & Refinery
Tata Consultancy Services Ltd.	Computers - Software & Education

Sector Allocation

Sector	%
Auto & Auto ancilliaries	7.14
Banks	10.12
Computers - Software & Education	6.04
Current Assets	27.75
Diversified	4.16
Electronics	1.99
Engineering & Industrial Machinery	3.56
Entertainment	1.49
Hotels & Resorts	2.06
Metals	1.53
Miscellaneous	4.34
Oil & Gas, Petroleum & Refinery	8.06
Pharmaceuticals	8.35
Power Generation, Transmission & Equip	4.82
Steel	1.90
Sugar	1.29

Telecom	3.90
Transport & Travel	1.49

Here, in fund manager's portfolio major investment is in bank, Oil & Gas, Petroleum & Refinery, Pharmaceuticals, engineering, auto sector.

Asset Allocation

Equity	Debt	Cash & Equivalent
72.25	0.00	27.75

In the above scheme, we can see that the asset allocation in equity is 72.25 where in cash & Equivalent is 27.75. So, the fund manager is diversion his risk in equity & cash.. We can also see that top 10 holding for the said scheme is in a volitale sector. So, Risk and return is also high.

3) Reliance Diversified Power Sector Fund

Objective

The primary investment objective of the Scheme is to generate consistent returns by investing in equity / equity related or fixed income securities of power and other companies associated with the power sector.

Fund Features

Type of Scheme	**Open Ended**
Nature	Equity
Option	Growth
Inception Date	Apr 15, 2004
Face Value (Rs/Unit)	10
Fund Size in Rs. Cr.	4521.63 as on Sep

	30, 2008
Fund Manager	Sunil Singhania .
SIP	✔
STP	✔
SWP	✔
Expense ratio(%)	1.81
Portfolio Turnover Ratio(%)	78

The said scheme is open ended scheme, so, investor can sell and purchase the units at any time. In this scheme, SIP, STP & SWP, all options are available for investment.

Top 10 Holdings

Stock	Sector
Other Equities	Miscellaneous
Reliance Industries Ltd	Oil & Gas, Petroleum & Refinery
Reliance Infrastructure Ltd	Power Generation, Transmission & Equip
Jindal Steel and Power Ltd.	Steel
Punj Lloyd Ltd.	Housing & Construction
Oil & Natural Gas Corp. Ltd	Oil & Gas, Petroleum & Refinery
Larsen & Toubro Limited	Engineering & Industrial Machinery
Bharat Heavy Electricals Ltd	Electricals & Electrical Equipments
Tata Power Company Ltd	Power Generation, Transmission & Equip
ABB Ltd	Electricals & Electrical Equipments

Sector Allocation

Sector	%
Banks	1.66
Current Assets	35.89
Electricals & Electrical Equipments	9.92
Electronics	1.77
Engineering & Industrial Machinery	8.36
Housing & Construction	6.48
Metals	2.40
Miscellaneous	8.90
Oil & Gas, Petroleum & Refinery	5.71
Power Generation, Transmission & Equip	14.66
Steel	3.04
Trading	1.22

Here the major part in fund manager's portfolio is Power sector, Nifty, Engineering & Electronics.

Asset allocation

Equity	Debt	Cash & Equivalent
64.11	0.00	35.89

Here asset allocation is equity & cash is 64:35 means fund manager's portfolio risk factor is less in compare to other scheme.

Chapter - 6

FINDINGS

These are the following criteria from which we gave the star to the particular scheme:

Return for the last three years (%)	Star
0-20	★
21-40	★★
41-60	★★★
61-80	★★★★
81-100	★★★★★

A)   Tata Mutual Fund

1) Performance of Tata Infrastructure Fund (G) (★★★ fund)

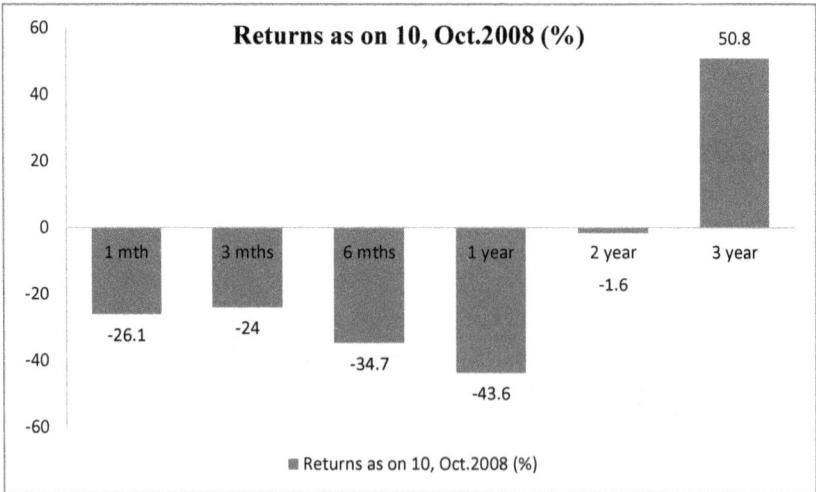

(Performance of Tata Infrastructure Fund)

Above table shows the returns in the different period. For the last one month, the Scheme gave the negative return and it was -26.1%. For the last 1 year, this scheme gave again negative return and it was -43.6% for the last 3 year, this scheme gave +50.8% returns.

e.g., one **invest Rs.10000 before 1 month**, then the **present value** of their money in negative and there is **7390**.

If he invest same amount of money **before 6 month**, then the present value of their money again in negative and there is **6530.**

If he invest same amount of money **before 3 year**, then he received 50.8%return on it and the present value of their money is **15080**.

So, from the return point of view the fund gave the better return.

If we compare the return of the all mutual fund for the last three years, then this scheme got the 4th rank.

2) **Performance of Tata Equity P/E Fund (G)   (★★ fund)**

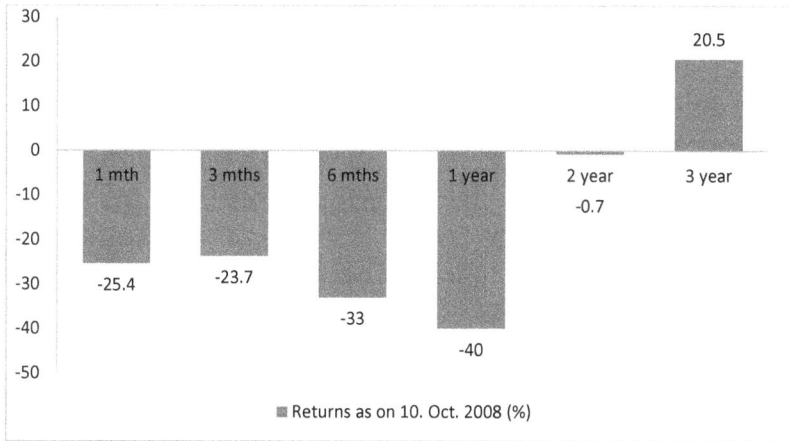

(Performance of Tata Equity P/E Fund)

For the last 1 month, the Scheme gave the negative return & it was -25.4%. For last 1 year, this scheme gave again negative return and it was -40% For the last 3 year, this scheme gave only +20.5% return ,means if one invest their money before 3 years then his\her money is increased by marginally 20.5%.

If we compare the mutual fund's return on the basis of the last 3 year return then this scheme got the 44th

3) **Performance of Tata Contra Fund (non rated fund)**

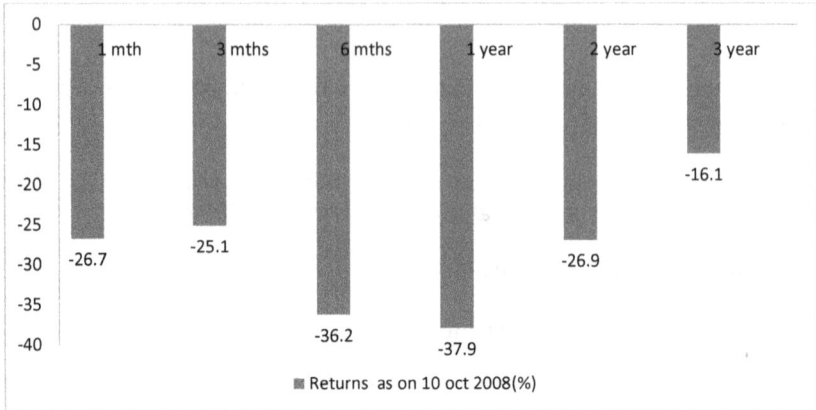

(Performance of Tata Contra Fund)

For the last 1 month, the Scheme gave the negative return & it was -26.7%. For last 1 year, this scheme gave again negative return and it was -37.9% For the last 3 year, this scheme gave only +20.5% return ,means if one invest their money before 3 years then scheme again gave –ve return and it was -16.1%.

If we compare the returns of the mutual fund for the last three year then the scheme got 110th rank among them.

B) Reliance Mutual Fund
1) Performance of Reliance Growth Fund - (★★★ fund)

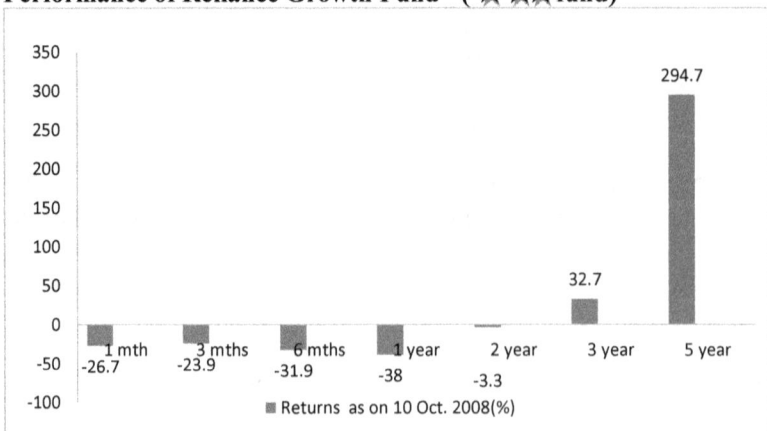

(Chart 13.4 Performance of Reliance Growth Fund)

For the last 1 month, the Scheme gave the negative return & it was -26.7%. For last 1 year, this scheme gave again negative return and it was -38% For the last 3 year, this scheme gave only +32.7% return ,and for last 5 year the fund gave +294.7% return   means if one invest their money before 5 years then their present value was increased 294.7%

if we compare the returns of the mutual fund for the last three year then the scheme got 22nd rank among them and,

If we compare the returns of the mutual fund for the last five year then the scheme got 2nd rank among them.

In comparison of the **last 5 year,** we like to give **5 Star** to this fund.

2) Performance of Reliance Vision Fund (★★★fund)

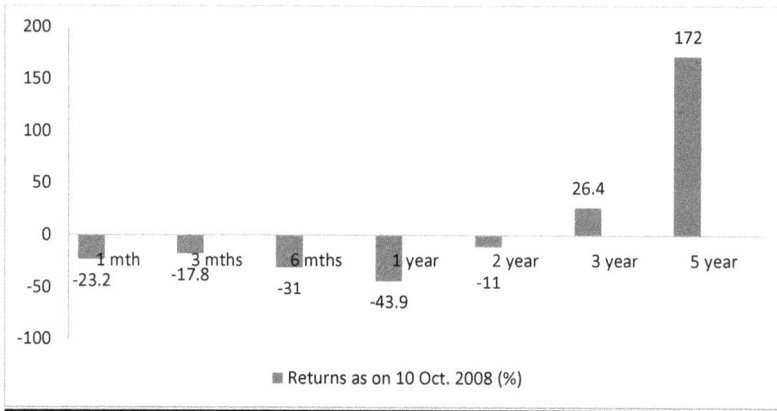

(Chart 13.5 Performance of Reliance Vision Fund)

For the last 1 month, the Scheme gave the negative return & it was -23.2%. For last 1 year, this scheme gave again negative return and it was -43.9% For the last 3 year, this scheme gave only +26.4% return ,and for last 5 year the fund gave +294.7% return   means if one invest their money before 5 years then their present value was increased 172% if we compare the returns of the mutual fund for the last three year then the scheme got 35th rank among them and,

If we compare the returns of the mutual fund for the last five year then the scheme got 23rd rank among them.

In comparison of the **last 5 year,** we like to give **5 Star** to this fund.

3) **Performance of Reliance Diversified Power Sector (★★★★★ fund)**

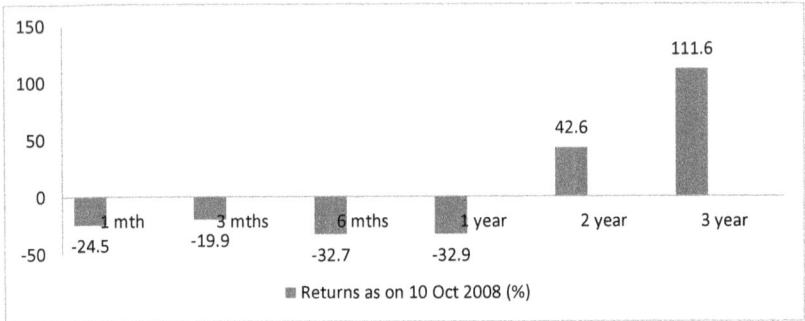

(Performance of Reliance Diversified Power Sector Fund)

For the last 1 month, the Scheme gave the negative return & it was -24.5%. For last 1 year, this scheme gave again negative return and it was -32.9% for the last 3 year, this scheme gave only +111.6% return. It means if one invest Rs.10000 before 3 year, then his present value of the money was Rs.11160

If we compare the returns of the mutual fund for the last three year then the scheme got 1st rank among them and,

If we compare the returns of the mutual fund for the last five year then the scheme got 1st rank among them.

In comparison of the **last 5 year,** I like to give **5 Star** to this fund.

Tools	Scheme					
	TATA			**Reliance**		
	Tata Infra.	**Tata Equity P/E**	**Tata Contra**	**Reliance Growth**	**Reliance Vision**	**Reliance Diversified**
Sharpe Ratio	0.31	0.32	0.23	0.35	0.28	0.44
Treynor Ratio	1.19	1.28	0.84	1.41	1.14	1.82

44

S.D. of Portfolio Returns	3.86	3.71	3.63	3.19	3.42	3.52
Beta of the Portfolio	1.01	0.93	0.84	0.80	0.80	0.85

(Comparisons between all six schemes of the Mutual Fund)

Interpretation:

1) The Sharpe Index of the TATA EQUITY P\E is higher than TATA CONTRA & TATA INFRA. The larger the Sharpe Index, the portfolio over performance the market and vice versa. So, from taking consideration of the SHARPE RATIO, "TATA EQUITY P\E" is better than "TATA INFRA." & "TATA CONTRA".

2) The Sharpe Index of the RELIANCE DIVERSIFIED is higher than RELIANCE GROWTH & RELIANCE VISION. So, from taking consideration of the SHARPE RATIO, "RELIANCE DIVERSIFIED" is better than "RELIANCE GROWTH" & "RELIANCE VISION".

3) The Treynor Index of the TATA EQUITY P\E is higher than TATA INFRA. & TATA CON"TRA. So from taking consideration of the Treynor ratio, "TATA EQUITY P\E" is higher than TATA INFRA. & TATA CONTRA.

4) The Treynor Index of the RELIANCE DIVERSIFIED POWER SECTOR is higher than RELIANCE GROWTH & RELIANCE VISION. So from taking consideration of the Treynor ratio, "RELIANCE DIVERSIFIED" is higher than "RELIANCE GROWTH" & "RELIANCE VISION".

Which one is better SHARPE or TREYNOR?

In the above example both the measures are giving exactly opposite performance evaluation of the funds. As per SHARPE Ratio RELIANCE DIVERSIFIED POWER SECTOR FIND has outperformed than others. After that Reliance Growth is better than others

If we consider only Reliance Mutual Fund then, as per SHARPE Ratio & Treynor Ratio,

1) Reliance Diversified Power Sector Fund
2) Reliance Growth Fund
3) Reliance Vision Fund

If we consider only Tata Mutual Fund then, as per Sharpe Ratio & Treynor Ratio,

45

1) Tata Equity P\E
2) Tata Infra
3) Tata Contra

But if we consider the whole Six Mutual Funds then, as per the SHARPE Ratio & the Treynor Ratio, they are ranked as under:

1) Reliance Diversified Power Sector Fund
2) Reliance Growth Fund
3) Tata Equity P\ E
4) Tata Infra
5) Reliance Vision Fund
6) Tata Contra

A clear understanding of standard deviation and beta will help us in solving this anomaly.

If one can compare the fund benchmark performance with the market than one should take Treynor Ratio as an appropriate measure for evaluating performance.

On the other hand if one is more concerned with the fluctuations of return from the portfolio over a period of time then one should take Sharpe Ratio as a reasonable measure as an evaluation criteria.

Chapter - 7
CONCLUSION & SUGGESTION

Conclusion

"Mutual fund is booming sector now a days and it has lot of scope to generate income and providing return to the investor, the mutual fund is one of the way to development of country and helps to mobilizing dead money in the economy which helps to develop the economic conditions of the country and people."

We also appraised investment performance of mutual funds with risk adjustment, the theoretical parameters as suggested by Sharpe & Treynor.

From that,

- ➢ SHARPE RATIO indicates that fund performance by considering overall total risk.
- ➢ TREYNOR RATIO shows that the fund performs well during 5 years of history and able to overcome the market risk.

The type of the study used in this project is based on **Secondary Data**.

Suggestion

Following are the suggestions for the both funds.

1) The fund house has to reduce the total risk involved in the fund in order to increase the return with good portfolio construction.
2) The fund house should select the innovative way of portfolio construction and should see the attracting areas of investing funds.
3) The fund houses should concentrate on the market conditions according to that they have to set the benchmark and invest in different sectors.
4) The fund houses should invest in good and attracting sectors to reduce standard deviation.

5) The fund house should try to reduce little more betas in order to generate more returns to investors.

6) The RELIANCE FUND HOUSE is investing in diversifies areas but they invest more in their own industries like (Reliance Industries, Reliance Infrastructure, and Reliance Communication) so, try to diversify their portfolio from which they reduce their risk.

7) TATA still reduce the standard deviation to generate more return by reducing total risk factors associating with mutual funds, and analyses all the factors.

8) TATA has to concentrate on those funds which are performing less than their benchmark return and take actions and analyze the market conditions and take correct steps

BIBLIOGRAPHY

Books:

1) Daniel K.(1997), "Measuring Mutual Fund Performance with Characteristics based Benchmarks" The Journal of finance, Vol-II, No.3,pp.1035-1058.

2) Dave, S. A. (1992) ,"Mutual Funds: Growth and Development" The Journal of the Indian Institute of Bankers.

3) Gupta LC. (1981), "Rates of Returns on Equities", The Indian Experience Oxford University Press, New Delhi, pp.5-17.

4) Henriksson, R. D. (1984), Market timing and mutual fund performance: An empirical investigation, The Journal of Business 57(1), 73–96.

5) Holthausen, Robert W. (1992), The prediction of stock returns using financial statement information, *Journal of Accounting and Economics*, 15 (3), 373 - 412.

6) Ippolito R A. (1992), "Consumer Reaction to Measure of Poor Quality: Evidence from the Mutual Fund Industry", Journal of Law and Economics, Vol. 35, pp. 45-70.

7) Jain PK,(1982), "Financial Institution in India –A Study of Unit Trust of India", Triveri Publication, New Delhi.

8) Jayadev, M (1996). Mutual Fund Performance: An Analysis of Monthly Returns. Finance India, 10 (1), 73-84.

9) Jobson J. and B. Korkie, (1981), "Performance Hypothesis Testing with Sharpe and Treynor Measures", Journal of Finance 36, 889-908.

10) Pathak Bharati V., "Indian Financial System" Pearson Education Publishing, New Delhi.

11) Ramola K.S. (1992), "Mutual Fund and the Indian Capital Market' Yojana, Vol. 36, No.11.

12) Rao, D. N. (2006), Investment Styles and Performance of Equity Mutual Funds in India. Available at SSRN: http://ssrn.com/abstract=922595 or http://dx.doi.org/10.2139/ssrn.922595

13) Sapar, Narayan Rao and Madava, Ravindran, "Performance Evaluation of Indian Mutual Funds". Available at SSRN: http://papers.ssrn.com/sol3/papers.cfm?abstract_id=433100

14) Sharpe W. F. (1966) "Mutual Fund Performance". Journal of Business, Vol.34, Issue 2, PP. 119-138.

15) Treynor J., (1965), "How to Rate Management of Investment Funds", Harvard Business Review, January-February 1965, 63-75.

16) Vyas ,B.A. (1990) "Mutual Funds- Boon to the Common Investors" Fortune India,.

Websites:

1) www.amfiindia.com/research-information/mf-history

2) www.icicidirect.com

3) www.moneycontrol.com

4) www.morningstar.com

5) www.mutualfundsindia.com

6) www.onlinemutualfund.worldpress.com

7) www.rediffmoney.com

8) www.reliancemutual.com

9) www.tatamutualfund.com

10) www.theeconomictimes.com

11) www.valueresearchonline.com

GLOSSARY

A

Annual Return: The percentage of change in net asset value over a year's time, assuming reinvestment of distribution such as dividend payment and bonuses.

Annualized Returns: Absolute returns over a period (which could be larger or smaller than a year) aggregated to a period of one year. Used for the purpose of comparing returns over different periods.

Applicable NAV: The NAV at which a transaction is affected. A cut-off time is set by the fund and all investments or redemptions are processed at that particular NAV. This NAV is relevant if the application is received before that cut-off time. If the application is received thereafter, it will be treated as the next day's application and allotted the relevant NAV.

Asset Allocations: Allocation of the funds held by the mutual fund to various categories of assets such as equity, debt and others. This is based on the investment objective of the scheme.

Asset Management Company (AMC): The Company vested with the responsibility of managing investments of the schemes of a fund in line with the stated investment objective of each scheme.

Automatic credit: The reverse of Automatic Debit. Saves the hassle of enchasing a cheque when withdrawing an investment. Your account is credited automatically with the amount withdrawn.

Automatic debit: Saves the hassle of writing a cheque when making an investment. Your account is debited automatically for the amount invested.

Automatic Investment Plan: Under these plans, the investor mandates the mutual fund to allot fresh units at specified intervals (monthly, quarterly) against which the investor provides post-dated cheques. On the specified dates, the cheques are realized by the mutual fund and on realization; additional units at the prevailing NAV are allotted to the investor. This inculcates a healthy and disciplined saving habit.

B

Back End Load: The difference between the NAV of the units of a scheme and the price at which they are redeemed. The difference is charged by the fund.

Balanced Funds: Funds that invest in equity and debt instruments in varying proportions. These funds supplement capital appreciation from equities with a steady return from debt instruments. To a large extent, the returns depend on the performance of the equity portion in the portfolio. There is some flexibility in changing the asset composition between equity and debt and fund managers exploit this to buy the best asset class at each time.

Benchmark: A parameter with which something can be compared with. For example, the performance of an equity scheme can be benchmarked against the BSE Sensex. In this case, the BSE Sensex will be known as the benchmark index.

Beta: It shows the sensitivity of the fund to movements measured against the benchmark. A beta of more than 1 indicates an aggressive fund and the value of the fund is likely to rise or fall more than the benchmark. A beta of less than 1 implies a defensive fund that will rise or fall less than the benchmark. A beta of 1 indicates that the fund and the benchmark will react identically.

C

Close-ended schemes: Schemes, which have a fixed date of redemption.

Custodian: Agencies, which have custody of all the securities purchased by the mutual fund. The service can be provided only by a person who has been granted a certificate of registration to carry on the business of custodian of securities under the SEBI regulations.

D

Debt / Income Funds: Funds that invest in income bearing instruments such as corporate debentures, PSU bonds, gilts, treasury bills, certificates of deposit and commercial papers. Although these funds are less volatile, the underlying investments carry a credit risk. Comparatively, these funds are less risky and are preferred by risk-averse investors.

Diversification: Investing in separate asset classes (stocks, bonds, cash) and/or stocks of different companies in an attempt to lower overall investment risk.

Dividend: Portion of profits that a company or a mutual fund distributes to its shareholders or unit holders.

Dividend Frequency: The periodicity of dividend payout of a scheme. This is especially valid in the case of an income/debt scheme.

Dividend Payout: In a dividend payout option, the fund pays out dividend from time to time as and when a dividend is declared.

Dividend Reinvestment: In a dividend reinvestment option, the dividend is reinvested in the scheme itself. Hence instead of receiving dividend, the unit holders receive units. Thus the number of units allotted under the dividend reinvestment option would be the dividend declared divided by the ex-dividend NAV.

E

Entry Load: The fee charged at the time of investment. It amounts to the difference between the NAV of the units of a scheme and the price at which new units are allotted on fresh investments. The fee has to fall within the overall limit laid down by SEBI.

Equity Linked Savings Scheme: A special product offered by mutual funds. As per the proposal put forth in the Union Budget 2005, subject to necessary parliamentary approvals, investments to the tune of Rs. 1 lacs in specified instruments are eligible as a deduction from gross total income under section 80 C. One of the instruments that are eligible for this deduction is an Equity Linked Savings Scheme (ELSS). Tax deduction for this investment is available at the marginal rate of taxation of the investor. The product therefore offers an investor the opportunity to invest in equity markets (which offer potentially higher returns) and at the same time avail of tax benefits.

Equity Schemes: Schemes where more than 50% of the investments are done in equity and equity related securities of various companies. These funds tend to provide maximum returns over a long-term horizon. However, the returns from these funds are directly linked to the stock market and are volatile as compared to those from debt funds.

Ex-dividend Date: In respect of any distribution of dividend, the date from which the holders are not entitled to the dividend. The NAV is accordingly reduced to the extent of the dividend declared.

Exit Load: The fee charged at the time of redemption. It amounts to the difference between the NAV of the units of a scheme and the price at which existing units are redeemed. The fee has to fall within the overall limit laid down by SEBI.

F

Fund: A mutual fund is a trust under the Indian Trust Act. Each fund manages one or more schemes.

Fund Category: Classification of a scheme depending on the type of assets in which the corpus is invested by the mutual fund company. It could be a growth, debt, balanced, gilt or liquid scheme.

Fund Family: All the schemes which are managed by one mutual fund.

Fund Manager: The person who makes all the final decisions regarding investments of a scheme.

Fiscal Year: A 12-month accounting period. From April 1st to March 31st.

G

Gilt funds: Funds which invest only in government securities of different maturities with virtually no default risk. While returns are steady and secure, they are generally lower than those from other debt funds.

Growth Option: A scheme where the fund ploughs back the dividend announced. The fund allots as many units of the scheme as are arrived at on dividing the dividend amount by the ex-dividend NAV.

I

Income / Debt Funds: Funds that invest in income bearing instruments such as corporate debentures, PSU bonds, gilts, treasury bills, certificates of deposit, commercial papers etc. Although these funds are less volatile, the underlying investments carry a credit risk. Comparatively, these funds are less risky and are preferred by risk-averse investors.

Index Funds: A class of equity funds that invest in equity shares of various companies in the same proportion in which they appear in the composition of any popular index, such as the BSE Sensex, S&P 500 or NASDAQ composite. The performance of such funds closely tracks the performance of the index.

Investment objective: The declared purpose of investment of a mutual fund scheme.

J

Jensen Measures: It measures the difference between market risk and actual performance of the fund.

L

Liquid Funds / Money Market Funds: Funds investing in short-term money market instruments including treasury bills, commercial paper and certificates of deposit.

Load: The fee charged by the fund either at the time the investor buys into the fund (entry load) or when he redeems his units (exit load). Funds that charge these loads at the time of entry or exit are called load funds. It amounts to the difference between the NAV of the units of a scheme and the price at which new units are allotted on fresh investments or existing units are redeemed. Though the load is decided by the AMC, it has to fall within the overall limit laid down by SEBI. Schemes that do not charge any load and are called "no-load" schemes.

Lock In Period: The period after investment in fresh units during which the investor cannot redeem the units.

M

Maturity: The specified date on which the units of a close-ended scheme are due for redemption.

Maximum Repurchase / Withdrawal: A time frame decided by the fund beyond which the fund will not entertain any application for redemption of units. This could be a day or a week or any other period.

Minimum Subscription: The minimum amount required to be invested to purchase units of a scheme of a mutual fund.

Minimum Withdrawal: The smallest sum that an investor can withdraw (get redeemed) from the fund at one time.

Money Market Instruments: As defined under the SEBI (MF) Regulations 1996 including Commercial paper, treasury bills, GOI securities with an unexpired maturity up to one year, call money, certificates of deposit and any other instrument specified by the Reserve Bank of India.

Money Market Mutual Funds/ Liquid Funds: These funds invest only in money market instruments including treasury bills, commercial paper or certificate of deposits of a very short-term maturity.

Mutual Funds: A mutual fund is a collection of stocks or bonds. This happens when a large number of people give their money to professionals, to manage and invest, with the aim of achieving a return. These qualified and experienced professionals invest in instruments according to the objective of the fund.

N

Net asset value (NAV): The value of a unit of a scheme on any given business day. NAV reflects the market value of the fund's investments that day after accounting for all expenses.

O

Objective of Investment: The purpose statement consisting of the goal and the avenues of investment specified by the fund in its offer document.

Open-ended Schemes: Schemes for which a fixed date of redemption is not specified. The fund offers to sell and buy units at any time at prices   linked to the prevailing NAV.

P

Performance: Performance of an investment indicates the returns from an investment. The returns can come by way of income distributions as well as appreciation in the value of the investment.

Portfolio: The basket of investments in which the funds of a scheme are deployed.

Price of Units: Price offered by a mutual fund for repurchase or sale of a unit on a daily basis.

Prospectus: An offer document by which a mutual fund invites the public for subscription to units of a scheme, and informs them of the terms & conditions for management of the scheme on a day to day basis thereafter. The document contains information about the scheme to enable a prospective investor make an informed investment decision.

R

Rate of Return: The difference between the prices paid for a security and the security's sale price including any cash distribution expressed as a percentage.

Redemption / Repurchase price: The price of a unit (net of exit load) that the fund offers the investor to redeem his investment.

Redemption of Units / Repurchase: Buying back/cancellation of the units by a fund on an on-going basis or on maturity of a scheme. The investor is paid a consideration linked to the NAV of the scheme.

Registrar: An agent appointed by the trustees of a mutual fund in consultation with the AMC or by the companies for the purpose of handling the records of the unit holders or shareholders.

Repurchase Date /Period: In the case of close-ended schemes, the specified date on which or period during which the investor can redeem units held by him in the scheme before the maturity of the scheme.

S

Sales charge: A charge added on to the price of a mutual fund when you buy it.

Sector funds: Schemes of mutual funds that invest predominantly in a particular industry or sector of the economy such as information technology, pharmaceuticals, FMCG etc. These funds tend to be more volatile than funds holding a diversified portfolio of securities across many industries, but may offer greater potential returns. These funds should be considered only if one has a relatively higher risk appetite.

Sharpe Ratio: Statistical measure of a portfolio's historic "risk-adjusted" performance. Calculated by dividing a fund's excess return by the standard deviation of those returns. This is a measure of return of a portfolio given the risk taken by it. The higher the ratio, the better the portfolio.

Standard Deviation: This is a measure of deviation or historic volatility of a portfolio. It measures the dispersion of a fund's periodic returns from its mean value. The wider the dispersion, the higher the standard deviation and thus higher the risk. Lower standard deviation is therefore preferred.

Stocks: Stocks represent a part equity ownership of a corporation. When someone holds stocks of a certain company, it means that he/she owns shares of that company and therefore becomes a part owner of that company in proportion to his/her holding. These securities generally have the most potential for capital appreciation, but their rights are subordinated in the event of a company liquidation or bankruptcy.

Switching: It is the transfer of one's investment from one scheme to another.

Systematic Encashment / Withdrawal Plan (SEP / SWP): A Systematic Encashment / Withdrawal Plan permit the investor to receive a pre-determined amount / units from his investment in a mutual fund scheme on a periodic basis. Retirees in need of a regular income often opt for this.

Systematic Investment Plan (SIP): A Systematic Investment Plan allows an investor to buy units of a mutual fund scheme on a regular basis by means of periodic investments into that scheme in a manner similar to installments paid on purchase of normal goods. The investor is allotted units on a predetermined date specified in the offer document of the scheme. Here the Plan allows the investor to take advantage of the Rupee Cost Averaging methodology.

Systematic Transfer Pan (STP): An STP allows the investor to transfer a pre-determined amount from his investment in a mutual fund scheme to another mutual fund scheme (of the same company) on a periodic basis. This Plan is generally used to transfer sums from a Money Market / Liquid / Cash scheme to another scheme.

T

Tax Deducted at Source (TDS): No tax is withheld or deducted at source, where any income is credited or paid by a mutual fund, as per the provisions of Section 194K and 196A of the Act.

Total Return: The performance of an investment, including yield (dividends, interest, capital gains) as well as changes in per unit price, calculated over a designated period of time expressed in percentage terms. Simply put, it is the return one gets on his investment taking all factors into account.

Trade Date: The actual date on which your units were purchased or sold. The transaction price is determined by the closing Net Asset Value on that date.

Transfer Agent / Registrar: An agent appointed by the trustee of a mutual fund in consultation with the AMC or by the companies for the purpose of handling the records of the unit holders or share holders.

Treasury bills (T-bills): A short-term debt instrument issued by the government with a maturity period of one year or less.

TREYNOR RATIO: This ratio is similar to the above except it uses beta instead of standard deviation. It's also known as the Reward to Volatility Ratio, it is the ratio of a fund's average excess return to the fund's beta. It measures the returns earned in excess of those that could have been earned on a riskless investment per unit of market risk assumed.

Trustees (of a mutual fund): SEBI requires all Mutual Funds to appoint a board of Trustees. They appoint and oversee the operations of the Asset Management Companies to ensure that the interest of investors is always safeguarded.

U

Unit: A Unit represents one undivided share in the assets of the Schemes.

Unit Trust: A special type of fund, usually a bond fund, that has a fixed portfolio, shares or "units" are sold when the fund is formed, and the portfolio remains fixed until the maturity of the underlying securities.

www.ingramcontent.com/pod-product-compliance
Lightning Source LLC
Chambersburg PA
CBHW071100280326
41928CB00050B/2568